TRAGEDY ON THE HORIZON

The Dred Scott Conspiracy
A Historical Narrative

Denise A. Pascale

PAGE PUBLISHING
Conneaut Lake, PA

First originally published by Page Publishing 2024

ISBN 979-8-88960-607-9 (pbk)
ISBN 979-8-88960-624-6 (digital)

Printed in the United States of America

To my mother, a lover of history
To my daughter, Amanda, and grandsons,
Keith Joseph and Raymond Thomas

If Slavery is not wrong, then nothing Is wrong!

—A. Lincoln

CONTENTS

FOREWORD

The Dred Scott Decision was read by Chief Justice Roger B. Taney on March 6, 1857. This decision had a major impact on the entire country because it said that the Negro could never be a citizen of the United States. Its consequences led to the election of Abraham Lincoln. Because Lincoln won, the Southern States seceded from the Union.

The tragedy of the Civil War was years in the coming! Of course the culture of slavery was engrained in the societies, both Northern and Southern States. Slavery was never to be extended into the new territories or states. The framers of the Constitution were very cautious about the way they handled slavery questions. They did not know how to present the Declaration's promise "that all men are created equal."

Here is my attempt to present the nature of the Dred Scott Decision, the worst decision of the Supreme Court's history. I have tried to prove that Senator Stephen A. Douglas spent his lifetime fighting for the nationalization of slavery.

This is a historical narrative. The discussion consists of a few theories for Abraham Lincoln in his debates with Stephen Douglas accusing him of planning with Franklin Pierce, James Buchanan, and Roger Taney, the Supreme Court Justice in the 1857 landmark Dred Scott Decision. We study history so that we can avoid repeating outcomes and save lives and prevent unnecessary wars. The purpose of this monograph is to prove or disprove this allegation. Was there a conspiracy or not? Much has been written; however, finding all the evidence to conclude these theories from over a century and a half was not possible. With all the technology we have today, e-mails, iPhones, and computers, it's hard to imagine that all Stephen Douglas or any involved in this plot had to do was throw away the original copy read from the bench.

The conspiracy starts because the Supreme Court is not supposed to be political. It's the third branch of government that should be impartial, to work clear of the passion of the current political issues at any given time. Decisions were to be based on principles of law. Lastly, Judicial rulings were not to be discussed with the presidents or in this case president-elect James Buchanan.

The following monograph presents theories about a historical event that is shrouded in history. It will take place with myself, the narrator, Professor Harris (fictional character), Thurgood Marshall (the first African-American Associate Justice), and Chief Justice William Rehnquist in a panel format as we watch the Lincoln–Douglas debates and the old Supreme Court where the Dred Scott Decision was read.

INTRODUCTION

Stephen Douglas was a short, stout man of about 5'3". He had a rather large head. He enjoyed bellowing and theatrics, thus the name the Little Giant. It is quite amazing that the Dred Scott Decision had already been decided a year before the famous debates. Slavery became national as Stephen Douglas engineered. So this is a recreation of the history, with me, the narrator, and my insights and interpretations.

In the panel commentaries, I agree with Professor Harris on some points and disagree on others. Professor Harris's opinions are also mine!

Douglas became familiar with slavery when his first wife died and was left a plantation in the territory of Mississippi. It didn't take him long to come to the conclusion that the Declaration of Independence and the Constitution were written for White people alone.

Lincoln-Douglas Third Debate

Jonesboro, Illinois
September 15, 1858

STEPHEN A. DOUGLAS. We are here today to devote time to the discussion of the political topics that now agitate the country. I'm sure most of you have heard Mr. Lincoln's House Divided speech. Mr. Lincoln's main proposition upon which he bases his claim in his own language is that this Republic cannot endure permanently divided into slave and free States, as our fathers made it. He says that they must become all one or all become slave and must be all one or the other or this government cannot last. Why can't it last, if we execute the government in the spirit and on the same principles upon which it was made? Surely Mr. Lincoln is a wiser man than those who made the government. Washington did not believe that the regulations, laws, and domestic institutions from the Green Mountains of Vermont were suited to the rice plantations of South Carolina. They believed then, and our experience has proved now, that each locality requires different laws; thus, our government was formed on the local laws and policy. Our government was formed on diversity, not uniformity.

Panel Commentary

Stephen Douglas only becomes familiar with slavery after his first wife dies. His father-in-law shows him the plantation lifestyle, and he learns fast how to twist his knowledge to benefit his political ambitions. He neglects to mention that the "institution" of slavery was to end after 1808 when the importation of slaves was to cease. We also know that George Washington could not have predicted that cotton would be the next free labor reason for slavery to flourish.

A Short Rebuttal from the Fifth Debate

LINCOLN. The Judge has alluded to the Declaration of Independence and insisted that Negroes are not included in that Declaration; that is a slander upon the Framers. I believe the entire records of the world, from the date of the Declaration of Independence up to within three years ago, may be searched in vain for one single affirmation, from one single man that Negroes were not included in that Declaration. I think I might defy Judge Douglas to show that he ever said so, that any president ever said so, and that any member of Congress said so, until the necessities of the present Democratic party, in regard to slavery, had to invent that affirmation!

Inauguration of President James Buchanan

On March 4, 1857, after a colorful parade, president-elect James Buchanan took the Oath of Office before Chief Justice Roger B. Taney. As President Buchanan thought that the upcoming Dred Scott Decision would finally end the slavery question, he gave his inaugural address.

PRESIDENT JAMES BUCHANAN. Fellow citizens, I appear before you this day to take the solemn oath that I will faithfully execute the Office of the President of the United States and will, to the best of my ability, preserve, protect, and defend the Constitution of the United States. In entering upon this great office, I must humbly invoke the God of our fathers for wisdom and firmness to execute its high and responsible duties in such a manner as to restore harmony and ancient friendship among the people of the several States and "to preserve our free Institutions through-out the many generations." Convinced that I owe my election to the inherent love for the Constitution and the Union, which still animates the hearts of the American people, let me earnestly ask their powerful support in sustaining all just measures calculated to perpetuate these, the richest political blessings that heaven has ever bestowed upon any nation. Having determined not to become a candidate for reelection, I shall have no influ-ence, my conduct in administering the government, except the desire, ability, and faithfully to serve my country and to live in grateful memory of my countrymen. The voice of the majority, speaking in the manner prescribed by the Constitution, was heard, and instant submission followed.

What a happy conception, then, was it for Congress to apply this simple rule (popular sovereignty) that the will of the majority shall govern, to the settlement of the question of slavery in the territories! Congress is neither "to legislate into any territory or State nor to exclude it therefrom, but to leave the people thereof perfectly free to form and regulate their 'domestic institutions' in their own way, subject only to the Constitution of the United States."

As a natural consequence, Congress has also prescribed that when the territory of Kansas shall be admitted as a State, it "shall be received into the Union with or without slavery, as their Constitution may prescribe at the time of their admission." The whole question being thus settled upon the principal of popular sovereignty—a principle as ancient as free government itself—*and finally, it's a judicial question that legitimately belongs to the Supreme Court of the United States, before whom it is now pending and will, it is understood, be speedily settled.*

To their decision, in common with all good citizens, *I shall cheerfully submit*; may we not then hope that the long agitation on this subject is approaching an end and the geographical parties to which it gave birth.

"Our free institutions throughout the many generations," of course, is how they describe slavery without using the word. All the historical accounts show that after the speech, President Buchanan met with Justice Grier to thank his long-time friend from Pennsylvania for his help. This is a major contribution to Buchanan's part of the conspiracy. Today, we would call it sins of omission.

Mr. Justice Catron and President James Buchanan wrote letters back and forth a few weeks before the final decision. They needed a Justice from the North to effectively let it look like the decision was not made South against the North. Justice Grier, a long-time friend of Buchanan's from Pennsylvania, joined the Southern Justices. My point of concern was that the three branches of government were not to communicate in regard to decisions that were being addressed in the Supreme Court before the decisions were made. *Separation of power was broken by these communications!* Thus, this was part of the conspiracy to nationalize slavery for all territories and new States!

Justice Grier delivered his short concurring opinion at the Old Supreme Court:

JUSTICE GRIER. I concur in the opinion of the court delivered by Justice Nelson on the questions discussed. I also concur with the opinion of the court as delivered by the Chief Justice that the act of Congress of March 6, 1820, is unconstitutional and void and the plaintiff cannot sue as a citizen of Missouri in the courts of the United States but that the record shows a prima facie case of jurisdiction, requiring the court to decide all the questions properly arising in it, and as the decision of the pleas in bar shows that the plaintiff is a slave, and therefore not entitled to sue in a court of the United States. The form of the judgment is of little importance, for whether the judgment be affirmed or dismissed for want of jurisdiction, it is justified by the decision of the court and is the same in effect between the parties to the suit.

By nullifying the Missouri Compromise of 1820, nationalizing slavery was made possible. The Dred Scott Decision basically stated that the Negro race could never be full citizens of the United States. They would always be a subclass, slaves or free, and would be allowed in all the States of the union. This means that they could never be allowed the total experience of their humanity! They could never be free to follow their dreams!

Yes, the world needs to be informed about all events that led up to the Civil War. The Framers of the Constitution expected that slavery would die a natural death after 1808. They never intended slavery to be allowed to continue and prosper. Slavery was the worst problem of the Constitutional Convention. These men knew that the Southern States would never join the Union; they could neither endorse nor oppose the "institution" of slavery. Slavery was written into the Constitution "such other persons." But where in the Constitution did it specifically say that slaves were property? Was it implied that slaves were property?

These and other questions were supposed to be decided by the Dred Scott Decision! *Actually this decision did what Douglas intended all along—it legalized slavery in all the new States and territories.*

The Lincoln-Douglas debates took place after the Dred Scott Decision and before the Civil War!

PROFESSOR HARRIS. To summarize what happened before this case came to the US Supreme Court, I give you the following facts: Dred Scott was a slave born in Southampton County, Virginia, in the late 1700s. In 1834, he traveled with his owner, Dr. Emerson, to Fort Sneed in the Missouri territory. The Missouri Compromise of 1820 prohibited slavery. Scott had no choice but to travel with his master, Dr. Emerson, who died shortly after. Dred Scott, with the help of his former owner Mr. Blow, filed a suit to buy his and his wife's freedom. Originally, the lower Court declared Scott to be free. However, the doctor's wife appealed against it, and it went to the Missouri Supreme Court. This is where the case became famous. Mrs. Emerson won. After that, she moved to Massachusetts and married Dr. Calvin Chaffee. who leaned toward abolition. She than gave custody of Dred Scott to John Sandford of New York. Roswell Field, Scott's attorney, then filed a new case in the US Circuit in Missouri. This led to the Supreme Court Case: Scott v. Sanford (the name was misspelled). *This case started the civil war.*

SCENE 5

Again I'm going to the seventh Lincoln-Douglas debate. Debates are in my own order to show a flow in the conspiracy.

LINCOLN. The other day I said, in answer to Judge Douglas, that three years ago, there never had been a man, so far as I knew or believed in the whole world, who had said that the Declaration of Independence did not include Negroes in the term "all men." I reassert it today. I assert that Judge Douglas and all his friends may search the whole records of the country, and it would be a matter of great astonishment to me if they shall be able to find that one human being three years ago who had ever uttered the astounding sentiment that the term "all men" in the Declaration did not include the Negro. *Do not let me be misunderstood.* I know that more than three years ago, there were men who, finding this assertion constantly in the way of their schemes to bring about the perpetuation of slavery, denied the truth of it. But I say with perfect knowledge of all his hawking at the Declaration without directly attacking it in the sneaky way of pretending to believe that the first man who ever said it was *Chief Justice Taney* in the Dred Scott case *not being born along by an irresistible current.* And next to him was our friend, Stephen A. Douglas. *Now it has become the catchword of the entire party.*

Now to describe the old Supreme Court house, it was small. On the back wall behind the bench was a fireplace, and over that was a large clock. The wall also had an arch over it with carved statues.

Roger Taney was the Supreme Court Justice. By the time he delivered his Dred Scott Decision, he was almost eighty and frail. He spoke in a very soft voice. His decision was about forty pages. Here,

I will use his original words without change or abuse. He read the whole opinion first.

Note: the original copy read from the bench was not preserved.

The first subject was the question of Scott's citizenship: Was he a citizen of the United States?

Old Supreme Court Chief Justice Roger Taney Reads Part of His Decision

The old Supreme Court house

Chief Justice Roger Taney. And upon a full and careful consideration of the subject, the Court is of the opinion that, upon the facts stated in the plea in abatement, Dred Scott *was not* a citizen of Missouri within the meaning of the Constitution of the United States and not entitled as such to sue in its courts and, consequently, that the Circuit Court had no jurisdiction of the case and that the judgment on the plea in abatement is erroneous. The words *people of the United States* and *citizens* are synonymous terms and mean the same thing. They both describe the political body who, according to our Republican institutions, form the sovereignty and who hold the power and conduct the government through their representative. They are what we familiarly call the *sovereign people*, and every citizen is one of these people and constitutes a member of this sovereignty. The question before us is whether the class of persons described in the plea in abatement compose a portion of these people and are not included and not constituent members of this sovereignty. *We think they are not, and they are not included under the word "citizens" in the Constitution and cannot therefore claim any of the rights and privileges, which that instrument provides, secures, and authorizes to citizens of the United States.* On the contrary, they were at the time considered a *subordinate and inferior class of beings*, who had been subjugated by the *dominant race* and were emancipated or not, yet remained subject to their authority, and had no rights or privileges but such as those who held power and the government might choose to grant them! The decision of that question belonged to the political or law-making power *instrument they have framed*, with the best light we can obtain on the subject, and to administer it as we find it according to due *intent and meaning when it was adopted.*

SCENE 7

Panel Commentary

Taney contradicts this sentence throwing it right back to the Congress. Taney's own distortion of the original intent of the slavery issue and Constitution seems impossible to me. In the 1842 Prigg v. Pennsylvania, then Attorney General Roger Taney ruled that free Negroes could not be subjected to "unreasonable seizure" or "deprived of liberty without due process of Law." He proposed a hypothetical case where a free Negro was on the street of Philadelphia and was seized by two citizens of Virginia and South Carolina, each claiming him as their slave. According to the position in Prigg's counsel, the state could do nothing to protect him. The District Court could not protect the free Negro's liberty; thus, this free man can be carried back into slavery. Taney sided with the North in the Amistad Case, which freed the Negroes and allowed them to go back to Africa.

From all I've read about Taney's previous decisions, he was not inclined to overstep or go into dealing with constitutional issues, usually called Judicial self-restraint.

THURGOOD MARSHALL. Why would he then decide to change his life-long constraint? I agree with you that Chief Justice Taney took the words "We the People" far too clear for anyone to think it did not include the Negro. So in 1842, Taney does admit that a free Negro has some rights as a person, citizen. In the above case, this free man was *Hamley Reasons*? I have looked at this case of course through my objective lens as the first African American Supreme Court Justice.

PROFESSOR HARRIS. I think there we see another clue to the outside help of a second person writing his opinion reversing the constitutionality of the Missouri Compromise of 1820. Douglas was a Circuit Court Justice before he was a senator; thus, he knew how to write Court Decisions. Stephan A. Douglas, the Little Giant, was the architect, the force behind nationalizing slavery. In 1847, Douglas was appointed chairman of the committee of the territories. He perpetrated the popular sovereignty idea years before the Dred Scott Decision. The Kansas-Nebraska Act side-stepped the Missouri Compromise of 1820, which forbid slavery in the northwestern territory. His motives were many. President Franklin Pierce wanted to pursue Manifest Destiny. To accomplish this goal, they both had interests in a railroad to cross to the Pacific. In later discussions, the Compromise of 1820 was built on the Northwest Ordinance of 1787. This fact is so infrequently mentioned. I would have thought that Lincoln would have used this argument to better his advantage in this debate.

THURGOOD MARSHALL. According to a quote by the historian James Schouler, "The repeal of the Missouri Compromise Was a 'plot' in which the chief conspirator was Stephen A. Douglas. Another historian said Douglas' goal was to win the Southern support for his rise to President. We need to go back and read some of the Newspaper accounts between December 1856 and March 7th 1857 when the final Dred Scott Decision was read. Here is one from the Washington Union, January 5, 1857." This case involves the constitutionality of the Missouri Compromise of 1820. The rumor is that seven of the judges, viz., Chief Justice Taney and Justices Catron, Daniel, Wayne, Campbell, Nelson, and Grier, decided that the law of 1820 be unconstitutional. It is certainly unusual for the intentions of the judges to leak out in advance. Scott claims to be free because he resided in Illinois, a free territory from which slavery was excluded. If Scott's claim to freedom, on this ground, is denied, we do not see how any State has the right to prohibit slavery. Slavery will thus become not only a *national institution* but the only one in which the sovereign States may not interfere.

Congress authorized one million dollars for the endeavor of the cross-continental railroad. At the head and front of the Northern effort for this line of course was Douglas. He was trying to connect the Great Lakes to the Pacific Ocean, just as he had *connected the Great Lakes to the Gulf of Mexico by means of the Illinois Central and the Mobile and Ohio railroads.* He had failed the latter scheme until he obtained Southern political support *through changing the bill so that it gave the south land grants as freely as to the north.* He again failed to get support for his bill opening up the Kansas to territorial settlement and statehood *until he let the bill have a rider that repealed the Missouri Compromise* (C. Sandberg, Vol. II, The Prairie Years).

Stephen Douglas defended the Taney Decision as necessary to overturn the Missouri Compromise of 1820. He defends the fact that the Supreme Court had to nationalize slavery. This was Douglas' plain all along with his misguided/deceiving use of popular sovereignty. This is the premise for my saying that Stephen A. Douglas wrote the Dred Scott opinion for Chief Justice Taney! This decision was *Judicial tyranny!*

SCENE 8

First Debate with Comparisons of Douglas and Taney Similarities

The first debate on August 21, 1858, was at Ottawa, Illinois. There was sweltering heat and huge crowds on horseback, ox-drawn wagons, fancy carriages, canal boats, and a train. Everybody stood, no chairs, only a few trees for shade.

STEPHEN DOUGLAS. The Whig and the Democratic parties jointly adopted the Compromise measures of 1850 as the basis of the solution to the slavery question in all its forms. Henry Clay was the great leader, with Daniel Webster on his right and Lewis Cass from Michigan on his left, sustained by the patriots in the Whig and Democratic ranks, in devising, adopting, and enacting the Compromise of 1850. Two-thirds of Congress voted against some of the elements of those assembled at Baltimore to nominate a candidate for president. They adopted the Compromise Measures of 1850 as the basis of action. Thus, the Whigs and the Democrats both stood on the same platform. The right of the people of each state and territory to decide their local *domestic institutions (slavery)* at the session of 1853–1854. I introduced into the Senate a bill to organize the territories of Kansas and Nebraska on that principle which had been adopted by the Compromise of 1850. Both the Whig and Democratic party in the National Conventions of 1852 endorsed the compromise, this in order that there might be no misunderstanding involved in the Kansas-Nebraska Bill. This put forth the true intent and meaning of the act in these words: It be the *true intent* and meaning of this *Act not to legislate slavery* into any state or territory, not to exclude it there from but to leave the people thereof free to form and regulate their *domestic institutions* in their own way, subject only to the Federal Constitution.

Panel commentary continues

THURGOOD MARSHALL. When Douglas wrote this bill, he intentionally left out the Compromise of 1820, 36°-30', which brought Dred Scott. By this action, he should have been free. Douglas had to be aware of these facts. Ruling on these political issues was not in the realm of the Judiciary system.

It is also worth noting that Mr. Douglas wrote the original and final draft of the 1850 Compromise intentionally leaving out that part of the 1820 Compromise that forbid slavery.

Douglas knew that the Missouri Compromise of 1820 also made Maine a free State without slavery. Was that also to be illegal after they denied the constitutionality of that document? Why was this not so obvious to all the other Justices? There was nothing in the Constitution about slavery being carried into the new States. As I have pointed out, the importation of the slave trade was to stop in 1808. Of course, the writers of the Constitution could not have predicted that after seventy years, the States would still be arguing and still treating slaves as property. *They were still considered three-fifths of a person. Property in humans should not have still been an issue in a civilized country.*

President Franklin Pierce in his inaugural address used the Constitution as his basis:

> I believe that INVOLUTARY SERVITUTE,
> as it exists in different States of this Confederacy,
> is recognized by the Constitution. I believe that
> it stands like any other admitted right, and that

States where it exists are entitled to efficient remedies ...

I believe that the constituted authorities of this Republic are bound to regard...

...Such have been and are, my convictions, and upon them I shall act. I fervently hope that this question (slavery) is at rest, and that no sectional excitement may threaten the durability of our institutions or obscure the light of our prosperity.

President Pierce says this and then uses God and providence as part of his "thinking!"

SCENE 9

The scene returns to Douglas, at the first debate

Douglas's style of speaking was distinct because of his size, 5'4". I'm sure it had to do with his ego demanding a loud and boisterous voice.

DOUGLAS. We are told by Lincoln that he is utterly opposed to the Dred Scott decision, and will not submit to it, for the reason, as he says, that it deprives the Negro of the rights and privileges of citizens. That is his main reason, he says, "for his welfare upon the Supreme Court of the United States, that it deprives the Negro of the rights and privileges of citizenship." (*The crowd applauses and laughs.*) Do you desire to turn this beautiful State into a free Negro colony in order that when Missouri shall abolish slavery, she can send us these emancipated slaves to become citizens and voters on an equality with you? If you desire Negro citizenship—if you desire them to come into the State and stay with white men—if you desire to let them vote on an equality with yourselves, *I believe that this government was made on the White basis. I believe it was made by White men for the benefit of White men and their posterity forever, and I am in favor of confining citizenship to White men—men of European birth and European descendants—instead of conferring it on the Negroes and Indians and other inferior races!* (*The crowds went crazy with excitement, cheering, "Douglas forever!"*)

DOUGLAS, *continues.* Lincoln and his abolitionist followers read the Declaration of Independence that all men are created free and equal and then says, "How can you deprive the Negro of that equality, which God and the Declaration of Independence award him?" They say that the law of God gives them equality.

I do not question Mr. Lincoln's conscientious belief that the Negro was made equal and hence his brother. But for my part, I do not regard the Negro as my equal, and I positively deny that he is my brother or any kin to me whatsoever. *I do not believe the Almighty has endowed him as our equal with the same rights. I do not believe that the Almighty ever intended the Negro to be the equal of the White man.*

Loud cheering
It took several minutes for the crowd to settle down

Does Douglas's words sound similar to the following? To the words of Chief Justice Taney?

CHIEF JUSTICE TANEY. It is very clear that no State can, by act or law of its own, pass *since the adoption Constitution* introduces a *new member* into the political community created by the Constitution of the United States. It cannot make him a member of this community by making him a member of its own. *And for this same reason, it cannot introduce any "person" or description of "persons."* The question that arises is whether the provisions of the Constitution, in relation to the personal rights and privileges to which the citizen of a State should be entitled, embraced the Negro African race, at that time in this country, or right afterward be imported, who had then or should be afterward be made free in any State and to put it in power of a single State to make him a citizen of the United States and endue him with full rights of citizenship in every other State without their consent? Does the Constitution of the United States act upon him whenever he shall be made free under the laws of a State and raised there to the rank of a citizen and immediately clothe him with all the privileges of a citizen in every other State and in its own courts? The court thinks the affirmative of these propositions cannot be maintained. And if it cannot, the plaintiff in error would not be a citizen of the State of Missouri, within meaning of the Constitution of the United States and, consequently, was not entitled to sue in its courts.

Associate Justice Benjamin Curtis, *dissenting*. Every free person born on the soil of a State, who is a citizen of that State, by force of the Constitution or laws, is also a citizen of the United States and consequently can sue a citizen of a different State in Federal court. The Constitution of New Hampshire conferred the elective franchise (right to vote) upon every inhabitant of the State having the necessary qualifications, *of which color or descendant was not one.* The Constitution of New York gave the right to vote to "every male inhabitant, who shall have resided and making no discrimination between free colored persons and others" (N.Y., Art. 2, Rev. Stats of N.Y. vol. 1, p. 126). That of New Jersey, to "all inhabitants of this colony, of full age, who are worth pounds Sterling 50 proclamation money, clear estate." New York, by its Constitution of 1820, required colored persons to have some qualifications as prerequisites for voting, which White persons need not possess. And New Jersey, by its present Constitution, restricts the right to vote to White male citizens. But these changes can have no other effect on the present inquiry, *except to show that before they were made, no such restrictions existed and colored, in common with White, persons were not only citizens of those states but entitled to the elective franchise on the same qualifcations as White persons, as they are now in New Hampshire and Massachusetts.* I shall not enter into an examination of the existing options of that period respecting the African race, nor into any discussion concerning the meaning of those asserted, in the Declaration of Independence, that all men are created equal; that they are endowed by their Creator with certain inalienable rights; and that among them are life, liberty, and the pursuit of happiness. My own opinion is that a calm comparison of these assertions of universal abstract truths, and of their own individual opinions and acts, *would not leave any of these men under any reproach of inconsitancy*; that the Great Truths they asserted on that solemn occasion, they were ready and anxious to make effectual, wherever a neces-sary regard to circumstances which no Statesmen can disregard without producing more evil than good, would allow; and that it would not be to just them, nor true to itself, to allege that they intended to say that the Creator *of all men* had endowed the White race exclusively, with great natural rights, which the Declaration of Independence asserts. As I conceive, we should deal here not with such disputes, *if there can be a dispute concerning this subject*, but with those substantial acts evinced by the written Constitutions of States and by the notorious practice under them. And they show, in a manner which no argument can obscure, that in some of the original thirteen States, *free colored persons, before and at the time of the formation of the Constitution, were citizens of those States.*

CHIEF JUSTICE TANEY, *continues a few paragraphs down to say that the language of the Declaration of Independence is equally conclusive.* We hold these truths to be self-evident—that all men are created equal; that they are endowed by their Creator with unalienable rights, among them are life, liberty, and the pursuit of happiness; that to secure these rights, governments are instituted, deriving their just powers from the consent of the governed! The general words above would seem to embrace the whole of human family and if they were used in a similar instrument today would be so understood, *but it is too clear to dispute that the enslaved African race was not intended to be included* and formed no part of the people who framed and adopted this declaration for if the *language as understood in that day* and would embrace them, the conduct of the distinguished men would have been utterly and fragrantly inconsistent with the principles asserted. They perfectly understood the meaning of the language they used and how it would be understood by others, and they knew that it would not in any part of the civilized world be supposed to embrace the Negro race, the brief preamble set forth by whom it was formed, for what purposes, and for what benefit and protection. It speaks in general terms of the people of the United States and citizens of the several states. The Declaration uses these terms so well understood that no further description or definition was necessary.

LINCOLN, *replies by reading from a speech he delivered at Peoria, Illinois, October 1854.* My intention in quoting this speech is to show my understanding that popular sovereignty applied to slavery does allow people of the territory to have slavery *and it doesn't allow them not to have it if they don't want it*!

This is the REPEAL of the Missouri Compromise. The foregoing history may not be precisely accurate in every particular; but I am sure it is sufficiently so, for all the uses I shall attempt to make of it, and in it, we have before us, the chief materials enabling us to correctly judge whether the repeal of the Missouri Compromise is right or wrong.

I think, and shall try to show, that it is WRONG, WRONG in its direct effect, letting slaves into Kansas and Nebraska and wrong in its prospective principle; allowing it (slavery) to spread to every other part of the WIDE WORLD, where men can be inclined to take it. This DECLARED indifference, but as I must think, covert real zeal for the spread of slavery. I CANNOT BUT HATE; I HATE IT BECAUSE OF THE MONSTROUS INJUSTICE OF SLAVERY ITSELF. I hate it because it deprives our republican example of its influence in the World—enables the enemies of free institutions, with plausibility, to taunt us as HYPOCRITES. It causes the real friends of freedom to doubt our sincerity, and especially because it forces so many good men amongst us ourselves into an open war with THE VERY FUNDAMENTAL PRINCIPLES OF CIVIL LIBERTY—CRITICIZING THE Declaration of Independence, and insisting that there is no right principle of action but SELF-INTEREST...When they (the Southern States) remind us of their constitutional rights, I acknowledge them, not grudgingly, but fully and fairly; and I would give them any legislation for the reclaiming of their fugitives, which should not, in its stringency, be more likely to carry a free man into slavery, than our ordinary criminal laws are to hang an innocent one but all this to my judgment, furnishes no more excuse for permitting slavery to go into our own free territory, then it would be for reviving the African Slave Trade Law. The law which forbids the bringing of slaves FROM AFRICA TO NEBRASKA.

I, therefore, think that there is no reason why the Negro after all is not entitled to all that the Declaration of Independence holds out, life, liberty, and the pursuit of happiness. I have no disposition to introduce social or political equality. My judgment is that a system of gradual acceptability will take a great deal of time.

Courthouse to Hear the Dissent of Justice Benjamin Curtis

The setting goes back to the courthouse where we hear Justice Curtis and the first part of his dissenting opinion. First a little background information: Justice Curtis so clearly analyzes the meaning of freemen in the Constitution. If Benjamin Curtis had been the Chief Justice, the Civil War might never have been waged.

JUSTICE BENJAMIN CURTIS. *I dissent* from the opinion pronounced by the Chief Justice and from the judgment, which the majority of the Court think it proper to render in this case. The plaintiff alleged in his declaration that he was a citizen of the State of Missouri and the defendant (Sanford) was a citizen of New York. It is no doubt that it was necessary to make each of these allegations to sustain the jurisdiction, either sufficient or insufficient, that the plaintiff was a citizen of the State of Missouri. The plaintiff objected (demurred) to the plea. The Circuit Court adjudged the plea insufficient, and the first for our consideration is whether the sufficiency of that plea is before the Court for judgment, upon the writ of error. The part of the judicial power of the United States, conferred by Congress on the Circuit Courts, being limited to certain described cases and controversies, questions whether a particular case is within the cognizance of a Court and may be raised by a plea to the jurisdiction of such court. When that question has been raised, *the*

Circuit Court must, in the first instance, pass upon and determine it. Whether the determination be final or subject to review by this Appellate Court must depend on the will of Congress, upon which body the Constitution has conferred the power, with certain restrictions—to establish inferior courts, to determine their jurisdiction, and to regulate the appellate power of this court. Circuit Courts have not been made by Congress, the final judges of their own jurisdiction in civil cases. When the plea was adjudged insufficient, the defendant was obliged to answer over. *He held no alternative. He could not stop the further progress of the case* in Circuit Court by a writ of error, on which sufficiency of his plea to the jurisdiction could be tried in this court, because the judgment was not final and no writ of error would lie. *He was forced to plead to the merits.* It cannot be true, then, that he waived the benefit of his plea to the jurisdiction by answering over. Waiver *includes consent.* Here there was no consent. And if the benefit of the plea was finally lost, it must be because the laws of the United States have not provided any mode of reviewing the decision of the Circuit Court on a plea, *when the decision is against the defendant. This is not the law.* Whether the decision of the Circuit Court on a plea to the jurisdiction be against the Plaintiff or the defendant, the losing party, the true question is not what either of the parties may be allowed to do, but whether this court will affirm or reverse a judgment of the Circuit Court on the merits, when it appears on the record, by a plea the jurisdiction, that it is a case to which the judicial power of the United States does not extended, and upon the demurrer (objection) to this plea, the question which arises is whether the facts that the plaintiff is a Negro of African descent, whose ancestors were of pure African blood and were brought into this country and sold as slaves, may be true, and yet the plaintiff be a citizen of the State of Missouri within the meaning of the Constitution and the laws of the United States, which confer on Citizens of one state the right to citizens of another state in the Circuit Courts. Undoubtedly, if these facts were taken together amount to an allegation at the time the action brought, the plaintiff himself a slave, the *plea is insufficient*. It has been suggested that the plea, in legal effect, does so aver (prove) because if his ancestor were sold as slaves, *the presumption is they continued to be slaves, and if so the presumption is the plaintiff was born a slave, the presumption is, he continued to be a slave at the time action was brought!* I cannot think such presumptions can be resorted to, to help out defective averments in pleading, especially in pleading in abatement, where the utmost certainty and precision are required (Chitty on PL., 457). That the plaintiff himself was a slave at the time of action brought is a *substantive fact*, having no necessary connection with the fact that his parents were sold as slaves. For they might have been sold after he was born, or the plaintiff himself, if once was a slave, might have become a freeman before the action was brought. To aver (prove) that his ancestors were sold as slaves is not equivalent in point of law, to an averment that he was a slave. If it were, he could not even confess and avoid the averment of the slavery of his ancestors, which would be monstrous, and if it be not equivalent in point of law, it cannot be treated as amounting thereto when demurred (objected) to, for a demurrer confesses only those substantive facts, which might be inferred therefrom by a jury! To treat an averment that the plaintiff's ancestors were African, brought to this country and sold as slaves as amounting to an averment on the record that he was a slave, because it may lay some foundation for presuming so, is to hold that the facts actually alleged may be treated as intended as evidence of other distinct facts actually not alleged. It is a *cardinal rule of pleading*, laid down in Dowman's case (Rep., 9b) and in even earlier authorities therein referred to "that evidence shall never be pleaded, for it only tends to prove matter of fact; therefore the matter of fact shall be pleaded. Or as the rule is sometimes stated, PLEADINGS MUST NOT BE ARGUMENTATIVE (Stephen on Pleading, 384)."

Panel Commentary, Dispute between Chief Justice Taney and Benjamin Curtis

PROFESSOR HARRIS. This is all well and good; however, you need more to tie this into your reasoning. Do you have any information as to why Justice Curtis wrote a letter to Taney for an official copy of his opinion?

NARRATOR. Yes, I do. In researching, I found original letters in Chief Justice Taney's handwriting to Justice Curtis. I researched the archives at the Taney Historical Society, and there also, I found and made copies of Justice Curtis's letters to the Chief Justice. I will quote from these letters the proof that Taney did not authorize the Court Clerk, William T. Canoll. He was ordered not to allow Benjamin Curtis copies of the original opinion. Taney's handwriting was rather hard to decipher, a long, angry letter from which I should quote, "if you can picture the Chief Justice scribbling his notes." They took a totally different approach to the question of the citizenship of the slaves. I'm almost positive this dispute was the reason for Justice Curtis resigning from the bench.

CHIEF JUSTICE TANEY, *writing his notes at his home in Maryland.* Mr. Curtis's application for a copy of my opinion, when I wrote the answer to his first letter was abundantly sufficient to justify the opinion, I then entertained and upon it I acted, the fact that he was of the minority (could not decipher a few words) if he did not himself suggest the rules seem to be as evident to admit or doubt but for the denial of the Judge. And if he is truthful in that denial, one must lose all faith in circumstantial testimony and however conclusive it may appear to be. The opinion of the Court was delivered on March 6 (1857). The dissenting opinion of Justice Curtis on Saturday, March 7, and on that day, the court closed and adjoined to the next term. On Monday, March 9, Judge Curtis left Washington and returned home and on the same day filed his dissenting opinion with the clerk of court.

NARRATOR, *continues.* Here I put forward the most important conspiracy theory of my findings. Justice Curtis has his opinion published in full in a Boston newspaper—by his own authority. The name of the Supreme Court clerk was Wm. Thomas Carroll, Esq. After the end of the 1857 term, Mr. Carroll also left Washington, DC. Justice Curtis knows that Taney directed the clerk not to let him have the copy he was probably entitled to as an Associate Justice. This leaves me to believe that there was the time necessary for Stephen Douglas to manipulate the original draft, or even for that matter, I am of the belief that he, Douglas, wrote the opinion of the court for Chief Justice Taney. What was the reason Taney was so angry at Curtis? Other letters between Justice Wayne and Justice Daniel and the Chief Justice also made it clear that they did not want Benjamin Curtis having the manuscript copy. Why? They all knew it was being revised. If all the Justices were equal, they should all have had access to the original document. This is very underhanded and more proof of conspiracy! There is a major inconsistency and a cardinal rule not to rule on an established law such as the Missouri Compromise of 1820 without total agreement of all the Justices. Taney's handwriting went on for many pages and became less legible. He repeated the same ideas several times (showing his inability to concentrate?). Taney was very intrigued by Curtis's motivation for wanting the whole opinion. Justice Curtis knows that Taney directed the court clerk not to let him have the copy he was entitled to as a member of the court! Was the Chief Justice hiding the truth? What's the reason for holding back on Curtis's copy of the opinion? I'm going to quote from Justice Curtis's letter: "You speak of my desiring the copy for some unexplained purpose. I did not think it necessary to explain to the clerk of the Court the purpose for which I wanted to see [a few words are not clear]. I thought it enough for me to say I had occasion to examine these papers. The clerk was simply directed not to comply with my request."

PROFESSOR HARRIS. This was most likely the only time they had for Senator Douglas and the Chief Justice to conceal the fact that Senator Douglas wrote the opinion and added the eight pages that were *not in the reading from the bench*! It is nowhere in the records that Douglas was at the courthouse the day of the reading! Why not? Another mystery! As was previously stated, the Lincoln-Douglas debates came after the Dred Scott Decision. Again, why did Stephen Douglas defend the court so vigorously?

SCENE 12

Seventh Lincoln-Douglas Debate

At the seventh Lincoln-Douglas debate, Lincoln quotes parts of a speech by Henry Clay, the famous Statesman:

It is a general declaration in the act of announcing to the world the independence of the Thirteen American Colonies, that all men are created equal. Now as an abstract principle, there is no doubt of the truth that the declaration, and it is desirable, in the original construction of society, and in organized societies to keep in view as a great fund: Unental principle. But then I apprehend that in no society that did exist, or ever shall be formed, was or can the equality asserted among the human race be practically enforced. There are portions—women, minors, insane people, culprits, transient sojourners—that will probably remain subject to the government of another portion of the community.

That declaration, whatever may be the extent of its import, was made by the delegations of the thirteen states. In most of them slavery existed, and had long existed, and was established by law. It was introduced and forced upon the colonies by the paramount law of England. Do you believe that in making that declaration the States that concurred in it intended that it should be tortured into a virtual emancipation of all the slaves within the respective limits? Would Virginia and other Southern States have ever united in a declaration that was to be interpreted into abolition of slavery among them? To impute such a secret and avowed purpose would be to charge a political fraud upon the noblest band of patriots that ever assembled in council-a fraud upon the confederacy of the Revolution-a fraud upon the union of those States whose constitution not only recognized the lawfulness of slavery, but permitted the importation of slaves from Africa until the year 1808. I have no concealment of my opinions in regard to the institution of slavery. I LOOK UPON IT AS EVIL...IF A STATE OF NATURE EXISTED, AND WE WERE ABOUT TO LAY FOUNDATIONS OF SOCIETY, NO MAN WOULD BE MORE STRONGLY OPPOSED THAN I SHOULD BE, TO INCORPORATING THE INSTITUTION OF SLAVERY AMONG ITS ELEMENTS.

LINCOLN, *continues with his own words*. I ask then to have the public eye turned upon it, if I ask, in relation to the organization of new territories and societies, this fundamental principal should be regarded, *holding it up to the public view and recognizing what Clay recognized as the great principle of free government.*

DOUGLAS. The Republican creed and platform point to Lincoln's "We cannot endure half slave and half free." Our founders designed the Union with slavery in some States and not others. Does Mr. Lincoln think he knows better than our founders? He then crusades against the Dred Scott Decision reasoning that it deprived Negroes of the rights and benefits in the Constitution of the United States, which guarantees to the citizens of each and every State all the rights, privileges, and immunities of the citizens of other States. He then took the ground that the Declaration of Independence having declared all men are equal and equal by divine right, the Negro equality was an inalienable right of which they could not be deprived.

This is the crux of the whole slavery issue. Slavery should not have even been an issue as the country expanded to the west. Douglas thinks he can twist the words of Lincoln and use them for his own benefit. So Douglas continues more words from Lincoln instead of his own. Douglas never sees the humanity of the Negro; he just considers them as part of an institution. Stephen Douglas works his popular sovereignty into his rhetoric with the end goal of defending the repeal of the Missouri Compromise of 1820.

Repealing the 1820 Compromise did what it was supposed to do: *extend slavery into the territories, thus nationalizing slavery!*

DOUGLAS. I than asserted what I believe to be a radical error. I repudiated it as slander upon the makers of this government. This government was made on the great basis of the sovereignty of the States—the right of each State to regulate its own domestic institutions (slavery) to suit itself—and that right was conferred with the understanding that inasmuch as each locality had separate and distinct in interests, each State must have different and distinct local institutions. Our fathers knew, when they made this government, that the laws and institutions were well adapted to the Green Mountains of Vermont, unsuited to the rice plantations of South Carolina. So the answer is yes, the territories do have the right to bring our slave property with us!

Supreme Court to Hear the Dissent of Justice McLean

We return to the Supreme Court readings. We proceed to Justice McLean who also dissented. Mc Lean can be described as a man with a receding hairline. He wears his hair mid-length, straight, and evenly cut.

JUSTICE MCLEAN. This case is before us on a writ of error from the Circuit Court for the District of Missouri. An action of trespass was brought, which charges the defendant (Sanford) with an assault and imprisonment of the plaintiff and also his wife, Harriet Scott, and Eliza and Lizzie, his two daughters, on the ground that they were slaves, which was without right on his part and against the law. The parties agreed to the following facts: in the year 1834, the plaintiff was a Negro slave belonging to Dr. Emerson, who was a surgeon in the army of the United States. In that year, Dr. Emerson took the plaintiff to the Army Post of Rock Island, in the state of Illinois, and held him there as a slave until the months of April or May 1836. At the time last mentioned, Dr. Emerson removed the plaintiff from Rock Island to another military post at Fort Snelling, situated on the West Bank of the Mississippi River, the territory known then as the Upper Louisiana, acquired by the United States from France and situated North of the latitude, 36 degrees, thirty minutes north of the State of Missouri. Dr. Emerson *held the plaintiff in slavery at Fort Snelling from the year 1836 to 1838.* In the year 1835, Harriet, who is named in the second count of the plaintiff's declaration, was the Negro slave of Army Major Talieferro. He was in charge of Indian affairs. He took Harriet to Fort Snelling and kept her there as a slave until 1836. He then sold her and delivered her as a slave to Dr. Emerson. She was also kept there until 1838. Dred, forty, and Harriet, seventeen, were married at Fort Snelling with the consent of Dr. Emerson. Eliza and Lizzie, in the third count of the plaintiff's declaration, are the fruit of the marriage. Eliza is now about fourteen. She was born on the steamboat *Gypsy, north of 36-30" and north of the "free territory" on the Mississippi River.* Lizzie is now about seven years old. She was born in Missouri on the military post called Jefferson Barracks. (*McLean refers to the facts by stating*) But it is said if the Court on looking at the record shall clearly perceive that the Circuit Court had no jurisdiction, it is a ground for the dismissal of the case. This is rather a sharp practice and one that is seldom if ever occurs. No case was cited as an authority, and not a single case precisely in point is rec-ollected in our reports. There is no averment (positive declara-tion) in this plea, which shows an inability in the plaintiff to sue in the Circuit Court. It does not allege that the plaintiff (Scott) had his domicile in any other State nor that he is a freeman in Missouri. He has averred to have a Negro ancestry, but this does not show that he is not a citizen of Missouri, within the meaning of the Act of Congress to sue in the Circuit Court. It has never been held necessary, to constitute a citizen within the act, that he should have qualifications of an elector (voter). Females and minors may sue in the Federal courts, as so may any individual in the State under whose laws his rights are protected and to which he owes allegiance. Being born under our Constitution and laws, *no naturalization is required*; one of foreign birth has to be made a citizen. The most general of the term citizen is a "freeman." Being a freeman and having his domicile in a *State* different from that defendant, he is a citizen within the act of Congress, and the Courts of the Union are open to him. By all rules of pleading, the defendant's council complained that if the Court takes juris-diction on the ground that the plaintiff is free, the assumption is against the "master."

Panel Commentary

PROFESSOR HARRIS. Master, servant, or slave—how can it be that one human being can *own* another? Even if the other is considered to be of an *inferior race*, how can this be happening in a democratic society? Slavery was to become unconstitutional after 1808 when the importation of the African slaves was supposed to have stopped. I seem to recall Mr. Lincoln in an earlier not well-known speech contradicted Judge Douglas's saying that "We do not want to turn our Great State of Illinois into a Negro-worshiping, Negro-Equality community! Illinois will always be 'true' to the Constitution and Union."

NARRATOR. Douglas said this after returning from Washington to Illinois. This was after he betrayed his constituents by accepting the Southern Congressional voters condition "to expressly repeal the Missouri Compromise."[1] The actual *Freeport Doctrine* by Stephen Douglas goes as follows:

> The next question propounded to me by Mr. Lincoln is, CAN THE PEOPLE OF A TERRITORY IN ANY LAWFUL WAY, AGAINST THE WISHES OF ANY CITIZEN OF THE UNITED STATES, EXCLUDE SLAVERY FROM THEIR LIMITS PRIOR TO THE FORMATION OF A STATE CONSTITUTION?

---

[1] Quote of Carl Sandberg, Vol. II, *The Prairie Years*. Stephen Douglas gave his speech on the Established law of the land. Northerners did not want slavery. They were content with the way things were. Lincoln listened to Douglas from the front row. The following day, Lincoln addresses the same group (ibid).

My answer emphatically is, as Mr. Lincoln has heard me answer a hundred times from every stump in Illinois, that in my opinion THE PEOPLE OF A TERRITORY CAN, BY LAWFUL MEANS, EXCLUDE SLAVERY FROM THEIR LIMITS PRIOR TO THE FOR-MATION OF A STATE CONSTITUTION.

Mr. Lincoln knew that I had answered that question over and over again. He heard me argue the Nebraska bill on that principal an over the State in 1854 and 1855, and in 1856, and he has no excuse for pretending to be in doubt as to my position on that question. IT MATTERS NOT WHAT THE SUPREME COURT MAY HEREAFTER DECIDE TO THE ABSTRACT QUESTION WHETHER SLAVERY MAY OR MAY NOT GO INTO A TERRITORY UNDER THE CONSTITUTION THE PEOPLE HAVE THE LAWFUL MEANS TO INTRODUCE IT, OR EXCLUDE IT AS THEY PLEASE, FOR THE REASON THAT SLAVERY CANNOT EXIST A DAY OR AN HOUR ANYWHERE, UNLESS IT IS SUPPORTED BY THE LOCAL POLICE REGULATIONS. Those police regulations can only be established by the local legislature; and if people are opposed to slavery, they will elect representatives who will by unfriendly legislation effectually prevent the introduction of it into their midst. If, on the con-trary, they are for it, their legislation will favor its extension. HENCE, NO MATIER WHAT THE DECISION OF THE SUPREME COURT MAY BE ON THAT ABSTRACT QUESTION, STILL THE RIGHT OF THE PEOPLE TO MAKE A SLAVE TERRITORY OR FREE TERRITORY IS PERFECT AND COMPLETE UNDER THE NEBRASKA BILL. I hope Mr. Lincoln deems my answer satisfactory on that point.

LINCOLN: Wherever slavery is, it has been introduced without law. The oldest laws we find concerning it are not laws introducing it but regulating it as an already existing thing. There are not enough ships and money to ship them all away. What then? Free them all, and keep them as underlings? This would better their condition. I think it would not hold one in slavery or free them and make them politically and socially our equals? Gradual emancipation? What we cannot do is let slavery spread North! *In as much as you do not object to my taking my hogs, I should not object to your taking your slave? Now I admit that this is perfectly logical if there is no difference between hogs and Negroes!* The South and North agreed to that law that made African slave traders as pirates and provide hanging as punishment! I now ask you about all the free blacks that are descendants of slaves; they would be slaves themselves but for something which has operated on their White owners. What is that something? Is there any mistaking it? In all these cases, it is your sense of justice and human sympathy continually telling you that the poor Negro has some natural right to himself—that those who deny it make mere merchandise of him, deserving of kicking, contempt, and death. And now who will you ask us to deny the humanity of the slave and estimate him only to a hog? Douglas called for the sacred right of self-government. What about the Negro? Was he a man? If he is not a man, in that case, he who is a man may, as a matter of self-government, do just what he pleases with them. *But if the Negro is a man, is it not to what extent a total destruction of self-government to say that he too shall not govern himself?* When the White man governs himself, that is self-government, but when he governs himself and also governs another man, that is more than self-government. *That is despotism!* If the Negro is a man, why my ancient faith teaches me that "all men are created equal!" What I do say is that no man is good enough to govern another man without his consent. I say *that this is the leading principle, the sheet anchor of American Republicanism!*

PROFESSOR HARRIS, *agrees.* We know that importing slaves did not stop exactly in that year. This begs the question, "Revolution free all people?" *Does not all mean all? Therefore,* Stephen

Douglas, Roger Taney, Franklin Pierce, and James Buchanan knew or should have known more and applied their moral and ethical considerations. They, as Supreme Court Justice, senator, and presidents, are supposed to rise above political consideration and apply the law with respect to the Constitution as they took their oath of office to do. *In people?* Carl Sandberg's biography of Abraham Lincoln accused the above four men of this conspiracy. This was their plan all along to *nationalize slavery.* Again, I will read a reaction from a Congressional member of the House of Representatives, originally a Whig (1840) and in the Senate in 1854. He was antislavery and voted against the Kansas-Nebraska Bill. His name was William Fessenden, and he says, "The Constitution does not Recognize slaves as property, nor protect them as properly." (*In my research, I could not find Fessenden's whole speech.*) Other noteworthy people of the time also accused the Supreme Court of conspiracy. Senator William H. Seward of New York was against the Dred Scott Decision. Seward is quoted as saying:

> The Dred Scott Decision had been manufactured by the Court at the instigation of the President, both forgetting 'that judicial upsursion is more odious and intolerable than any other among the manifold practices of "tyranny." The "whisperings" between Buchanan and Taney at the inauguration thus confirmed an agreement already reached to hang THE MILESTONE OF SLAVERY ON THE PEOPLE OF KANSAS.
>
> The next day the President received the justices. Then on the next day, the Court rendered its decision, and the President having organized this formidable judicial battery at the Capitol, was now ready to begin the work of subduing Kansas through the 'fraudulent agency of the Lecompton convention.

William H. Steward had been against slavery his entire political career. In 1838, when he was Governor of New York, he refused to return three Negro seamen to the state of Virginia. In 1848, he said slavery must be abolished totally. He opposed the Compromise of 1850. He went on to become a leader in the new Republican party and ran against Lincoln for the presidency. Because of his stand against Chief Justice Taney and antislavery, I would suspect he was appointed to Secretary of State in Lincoln's Cabinet.

Roger Brooke Taney
(1777-1864)

Roger Brooke Taney was born March 17, 1777 on the Taney Plantation along the Patuxent River, in Maryland's Calvert County. The Taney family had come to the colony as indentured servants in the mid-seventeenth century but, after serving out their term of servitude, they later established themselves as prosperous tobacco farmers in the rich agrarian economy of southern Maryland. Taney grew up as a Maryland Roman Catholic with rural gentry privilege, was educated privately and then entered Dickinson College in Carlisle, Pennsylvania in 1792.

While at Dickinson, Taney came under the tutelage of Dr. Charles Nisbet, arguably one of the greatest educators of his day. If the correspondence between Nisbet and Taney's father throughout 1792-1795 are any indication, the Principal became almost a surrogate father to the young and talented student. Taney was a leading member of the Belles Lettres Society and graduated as *valedictorian* of the twenty-four students in the class of 1795. This honor he always valued since the students themselves at the time were responsible for such selection.

Taney studied law under Judge Jeremiah Townley Chase in Annapolis before being admitted to the Maryland bar on June 19, 1799. After a brief time as a Federalist state representative, he began his legal career in earnest in Frederick, Maryland. There he also met and married Anne Phoebe Charlton Key, the sister of Francis Scott Key, in January, 1806. The couple would have six daughters.

Taney was elected to the Maryland State Senate in 1816 and came to dominate the state's Federalists. By 1820 he had also established himself as one of the leading attorneys in Maryland and in September, 1827 accepted the position of State Attorney General. As the Federalist Party faded away, Taney looked for other political outlets. He had always been an avid supporter and admirer of General Andrew Jackson, acting as chairman of the Jackson Central

Illustrator John D. Whiting (b. 1884) captured the striking difference in height between Abraham Lincoln and Stephen A. Douglas in this oil painting of their encounter at Ottawa, Quincy, or Alton—the three debates that occurred in town squares much like the one depicted here. However, the artist erred in depicting Lincoln in his presidential-style finery; eyewitnesses to the debates commented frequently on his "grotesque" appearance and ill-fitting clothes. (From the Frank J. and Virginia Williams Collection of Lincolniana; photograph by Mary Murphy)

THE PRAIRIE POLITICIAN: STEPHEN A. DOUGLAS
In his early years in Illinois politics

SCENE 15

Supreme Court Partial Opinions of Justice Catron and Nelson

Old Supreme Court

We go back to the reading of the Justices. We will go to Justice John Catron, who also goes with the same "African descendant reasoning."

JUSTICE CATRON. Because Dred Scott was a Negro descendant of Africans who had been imported and sold in this country as slaves and thus had no capacity as a citizen of Missouri to maintain a suit in the Circuit Court. The plaintiff claims to have acquired property in himself and became free, by being kept in Illinois during two years. The Constitution, laws, and policy of Illinois are somewhat peculiar respecting slavery. Unless the master becomes an inhabitant of the State, the slaves he takes there do not acquire their freedom, and if they return with the master to the slave State of his domicile, they cannot assert their freedom after they return. I refer to the opinion of my brother Nelson, with which I not only concur, but think his opinion is the most conclusive argument on the subject to my knowledge.

NARRATOR. As you read the words of Nelson, they are exactly the same as *our senator from Illinois——Senator Stephen A. Douglas!* Douglas wrote the Kansas-Nebraska Act of 1854. It is my opinion that Douglas wrote much of the opinion of Chief Justice Taney, or Taney used the language from Douglas's previous Lecompton and other documents. We must also remember that Taney was old and frail. Was he capable of writing a forty-four-page opinion?

JUSTICE NELSON. The question upon the merits, in general terms, is the removal of the plaintiff, Scott, who was a slave with his master, from the State of Missouri to the State of Illinois with a view of temporary residence. The argument against these decisions is that the laws of Illinois forbidding slavery within her territory had the effect to set the slave free while residing in that State and to impress upon him the condition and status of a freeman and that, by force of the laws, this status and condition accompanied him on his return to the Slave State, and of consequence, he could not be there held as a slave, and after such residence and return to the slave State, such residence in the free State works as an emancipation. As appears from an agreed statement of facts, this question has been before the State of Missouri and a judgment rendered that this residence in the free state has no such effect but, to the contrary, that his original condition continued unchanged. The court below, the Circuit Court of the United States for Missouri in which this suit was afterward brought, followed the decision of the State court and rendered a like judgment against the plaintiff. In conclusion, our opinion is that the question is one that belongs to each state to decide, either by its legislation or Court of Justice and hence in respect to the case before us. To the State of Missouri, a question exclusively of Missouri law, and which determined by that state, it is the duty of the Federal courts to follow it. In other words, except in cases where the power is restrained by the Constitution, the law of the state is supreme over the subject of slavery within its jurisdiction. Every state or nation possesses an exclusive sovereignty and jurisdiction within her own territory; her laws affect and bind all *property and persons residing in it.* It (the State) may regulate the manner and circumstances that *property* (slaves) is held. It is equally true that no state or nation can effect or bind *property out of its* territory. No State therefore can enact laws to operate beyond its own dominion.

Justice McLean, *dissenting. A slave is not mere chattel. He bears the impress of his maker and is amenable to the laws of God and man, and he is destined to an endless existence.* Under this head, I shall chiefly on the decisions of the Supreme Courts of the Southern States, especially of the State of Missouri. In the first and second sections of the sixth article of the Constitution of Illinois, it is declared that neither slavery nor involuntary servitude shall hereafter be introduced into this State, otherwise than for punishment of crimes whereof the party shall have been duly convicted; and in the second section, it is declared that any violation of this article shall effect the emancipation of such person his obligation to service. In Illinois, a right of transit through the State is given to the master with his slaves. This matter, as I suppose, belongs exclusively to the State. The first slave case decided by the Supreme Court of Missouri, contained in the reports, was Winny v. Whitesides (I Missouri Rep., 473) at term, 1824. It appeared that more than twenty-five years before, the defendant, with her husband, had removed from Carolina to Illinois and brought with them the plaintiff and that they continued to reside in Illinois three or four years, retaining the plaintiff as a slave; after which, they moved to Missouri, taking her with them. The court held that if a slave be detained in Illinois until he be entitled to freedom, *the right of the owner does not revive when he finds the Negro in a slave State*, that when a slave is taken to Illinois by his owner, who takes up residence there, the slave is entitled to freedom.

Panel Commentary

PROFESSOR HARRIS. This argument is all well and good, except that most slaves were illiterate, could not read, or did not know the laws until the conditions had passed—making it impossible for any slave to know what rights he did or did not have.

NARRATOR. There were several Missouri cases almost identical in the fact that slaves came to Army bases, even Fort Snelling where Dred Scott was held as a slave. These cases ruled for the slave being entitled to their freedom. The question of one State enforcing the rule of another State was the next step in enforcing the Constitution; it's called comity. Dred Scott was the only case that was appealed to the Supreme Court. The Federal court needed to finally rule regarding the freedom of these slaves to be free wherever they lived. *The Civil War would have been avoided!* In regard to Justice Peter Daniel, on January 3, 1857, his wife died in a fire while cooking in the kitchen. She was burned to death. The court postponed the Dred Scott Decision to give him time to grieve. They took up the questions again on February 7, 1857. Next we go to Justice Peter Daniel. He was also pro-slavery. He, like all the other concurring Justices, used that phrase that must have been agreed by them to give their case consistency of wording: "Dred Scott was a Negro of African decent, and that his ancestors were of pure African Blood, and were brought into This country and sold as Negro slaves."

The Old Courthouse

Justice Peter Daniel. To my mind, a conclusive reply to this singular argument is presented in the fact that the language of the Constitution restricts the jurisdiction of the courts to cases in which the parties shall be citizens and is entirely silent with respect to residence. A second answer to this strange and latitudinous (interpretation) notion is that it so far stultifies (renders ineffectual) the sages by whom the Constitution was framed as to impute to them ignorance of material distinction existing between citizenship and mere residence and domicile and of the well-known facts that a person, confessedly an alien, may be permitted to reside in a country in which he can possess no civil or political rights, or of which he is neither a citizen nor subject, and for certain purposes, a man may have a domicile in different countries, in no one of which he is an actual personal resident. The correct conclusions upon the question here considered would seem to be these:

> That in the establishment of the several communities now the States of this Union, and in the formation of the Federal Government, the African was not deemed politically a person. He was regarded and owned in every State as mere property, and was not and could not be a party or an actor, much less a peer in any compact or form of government, he has been or could have been elevated to the possession of political rights or powers, this result could have

been effected by no authority less potent than that of the sovereignty. The State exerted to that end, either in the form of legislation or in some other mode of operation, IT COULD CERTAINLY NEVER HAVE BEEN ACCOMPLISHED BY THE WILL OF AN INDIVIDUAL OPERATING INDEPENDENTLY OF THE SOVEREIGN POWER. And even contravening and controlling that power. THAT SO FAR AS RIGHTS AND IMMUNITIES APPERTAINING TO CITIZENS HAVE BEEN DEFINED AND SECURED BY THE CONSTITUTION AND THE LAWS OF THE UNITED STATES, THE AFRICAN RACE IS NOT AND NEVER WAS RECOGNISED EITHER BY THE LANGUAGE OR PURPOSES OF THE FORMER; AND IT HAS BEEN EXPRESSLY EXCLUDED BY EVERY ACT OF CONGRESS PROVIDING FOR THE CREATION OF CITIZENS BY NATURALIZATION.

These laws, as has already been remarked, being restricted to *free White aliens exclusively*.

Panel Discussion

Narrator. In reading Justice Daniel's full opinion, he goes into a long history of the Roman Empire's laws in regard to slavery. At this point, he seems to show examples of one theory and then a reverse theory. Daniel quotes from Edward Gibbon's *History of the Decline and Fall of the Roman Empire*:

> In the decline of the Roman Empire, the proud distinctions of the republic were gradually abolished; and the reason or instinct of Justinian completed the simple form of an absolute monarchy. The emperor could not eradicate the popular reverence which always waits on the possession of hereditary wealth or the memory of famous ancestors. He delighted to honor with titles and emoluments his generals, magistrates and senators and his precarious indulgence communicated some rays of their glory to their wives and children. BUT IN THE EYE OF THE LAW—ALL ROMAN CITIZENS WERE EQUAL, AND ALL SUBJECTS OF THE EMPIRE WERE CITIZENS OF ROME. The first Caesars had scrupulously guarded the distinction of ingenuous and servile birth which was decided by the condition of the mother. The slaves who were liberated by a generous master immediately entered the middle class of libertine or freedmen. Justinian respected the rights of patrons, his indulgence removed the badge of

> disgrace from the two inferior orders of freed-
> men; whoever ceased to be a slave, obtained
> without reserve or delay the station of CITIZEN;
> AND AT LENGTH THE DIGNITY OF AN INGENUOUS
> BIRTH WAS CREATED OR SUPPOSED BY THE OMNIP-
> OTENCE OF THE EMPEROR.

PROFESSOR HARRIS. The Justinian Code was a body of Roman law by the emperor Justinian, the start of jurisprudence. Justice Daniel compares the rights of nations as independent and equal to each of the States in the Union. States of the United States are not equal to an independent nation. This could not have been logical then or now. Obviously, I understand States rights verses Federal Constitutional laws. Chief Justice Taney and the concurring Justices deemed that States could confer citizenship; it was not equal to Federal citizenship. This was the key to the Conspiracy.

NARRATOR. There were several Missouri cases almost identical in the fact that slaves came to any bases even at Fort Snelling where Dred Scott was held as a slave. These cases ruled for the slave being entitled to their freedom. The question of one State enforcing the rule of another State was the next step in enforc-ing the Constitution; the term is called comity. In my opin-ion, this is why the Dred Scott Case had to go to the Supreme Court. Another expert on this case was William H. Rehnquist, Chief Justice of the Supreme Court from 1987 to 2005. He was on the court when Thurgood Marshall was appointed.

(This scene will be like a conversation between Professor Harris quoting Chief Justice Rehnquist and myself, the narrator.)

CHIEF JUSTICE REHNQUIST. The Missouri state courts decided an important question of Missouri law but was scarcely of earth-shaking consequences. They ruled that Scott's sojourn in free territory and in a free state did not elevate him from his status as a slave when he returned to Missouri. After the conclusion of this state lawsuit, Dred Scott brought suit in Federal court against John Sanford, Mrs. Emerson's brother, claiming to be in Federal court by reason of "diversity of citizenship." Since Scott was still alive, he could not be a "citizen" of any state for the purposes of Federal jurisdiction. It was this ruling that Dred Scott appealed to the Supreme Court. But now another wrinkle appeared in the case. Part of his claim was based on his residence in Wisconsin territory, where the status of slavery was governed by the Missouri Compromise of 1820. Remember that all this happened before the Compromise was replaced in 1850—the Missouri Compromise provided that slavery was forever prohibited in the United States territories north of the parallel that formed the southern boundary of the State of Missouri. If the Supreme Court should deem it desirable, it could make the case not a relatively simple one turning on the law of Missouri but a very complicated and important one involving the authority of Congress to prohibit slavery in the territories that had not yet been admitted to the Union as States. From Lincoln's second debate, he said "as I may begin to say now, of charging as a matter of belief, that in the introduction of the Nebraska Bill into Congress there was a conspiracy to make slavery perpetual and national." On several occasions, Lincoln *declared that Congress had the power to stop the extension of slavery into the territories.*

PROFESSOR HARRIS. Stephen Douglas replies, "Thus you see that up to 1854, when the Kansas-Nebraska bill whose Popular sovereignty provisions were passed; this was why Mr. Lincoln was aroused to re-enter Politics."

NARRATOR. Well, you referred earlier to newspaper articles of the day. I found one from January 6, 1854. The *New York Tribune* says exactly that:

> An overt attempt is set on foot in Mr.
> Douglas's Nebraska bill to override the Missouri

Compromise. Hence he proceeds to incorporate the following provision: "When received into the Union 'with or without slavery' as their Constitution may proscribe at the time of their admission."

The article insinuates that Franklin Pierce was in agreement with Douglas. They go on to say:

The acts of public men who place success before principle, anything but unmanly submission to slave power. If General Taylor had lived, and the Wilmot Proviso doctrine had triumphed, as it would have done through the instrumentality of his policy relative to our Mexican acquisitions, then we should have seen the reverse. Instead of finding Mr. Douglas down on his marrow-bones at the feet of slavery, we should see the same man standing up firm and strong in behalf of the glorious old Ordinance of 1787. FREEDOMS BATTLES WAS FOUGHT AND LOST IN 1850 AND THE COWARDS AND TRAITORS HAVE ALL RUN TO THE WINNING SIDE. LET THE COUNTRY TAKE NOTICE THAT THIS CONVULSION IS NOT COMMENCED OF THE SIDE OF FREEDOM.

The Northwest Ordinance of 1787 did forbid slavery. Thus, it makes sense that free blacks were citizens. Abraham Lincoln said that this ordinance to his mind successfully proved that the founding fathers did not want slavery to be extended into any new States or territories.

PROFESSOR HARRIS. Southern appellate courts agreed that a free Negro had some fundamental rights but not all the rights of a White man. Although Article 4, Section 2 states that "The citizens of each State shall be entitled to all privileges and immunities in the several States."

NARRATOR. When I started my research, it seemed to me that this was why the Negro was a citizen within the meaning of the Constitution. I realize that it's easy today to come to that conclusion. Why we had to fight a Civil War and have an Amendment to the Constitution can only be realized in hindsight. As I've said previously, slavery was not to be extended past the thirteen original States. Missouri was not included in the Ordinance of 1787, which was ratified by the Constitutional Convention. The Northwest Ordinance of 1787 was supposed to be the model for all the new States and territories. Another purpose was to admit all new States on an equal basis with the original. Our Congress governed the territory. This brings to question of how Chief Justice Taney claimed that Congress could not rule on the territories, why he deemed it necessary to reverse the Missouri Compromise of 1820! This brings us back to Stephen Douglas who in December 1847 proposed that "popular sovereignty" should or should not exist in the territories. Coincidentally, Douglas became Chairman of House Committee on Territories. So far, as Congress's power was concerned, Cass took the position that the "Constitutional clause referred to 'territory' only as property, and conferred no right of territorial political control upon congress. Consequently the Federal legislative power in the territories was strictly limited to the creation of proper Territorial Governments, and making provision for their eventual admission to the Union as States." Cass, in the Congress, insisted the people must be left to regulate such internal affairs (slavery) as they saw fit. "Even if Congress had the right to regulate such internal affairs of a territory, which Cass denied, he argued that would cause discord."

First Debate Again, Lincoln's Charge of Conspiracy

As we return to the first debate, I am making a clear charge of conspiracy

LINCOLN. I will state that my understanding is that *popular sovereignty*, applied to the question of slavery and as now applied… When I made my speech at Springfield [that speech of which the judge complains, or from which he quotes, "why"], I really was not thinking of this thing that he ascribes to me at all. I had no thought in the world that I was doing anything to bring about the absolute equality of White and black races. It never occurred to me that I was doing anything to reduce to a dead uniformity all the local institutions of the states, but I must say in justice to the judge that if I am really doing something that leads to these bad results, it is just as bad to the country, whether I wished it or not, but I ask you, on the basis upon which our fathers placed it, that it can have any tendency to compel the people of Vermont to raise sugarcane because they can cut it, the people of Grand Prairie to cut pine logs off the prairie where none grow because they can cut them in Maine? The judge does not generally claim that he is administering, by his Kansas-Nebraska doctrine, the slavery question upon the basis of the original Constitution. I think he says, in one of his speeches, that he saw evidences of a policy to allow slavery to be in existence South of a certain line. Now, I am fighting him upon this original principle. I am fighting in favor of "the old principle" of Washington, Jefferson, and Madison. Now, my friends, I want to attend a little to one or two other things. In that Springfield speech, my main object was to show so far as my humble self was capable of doing to arouse this country to the belief that there was a tendency, if not a conspiracy, to make slavery perpetual and universal in this Union, and having made that speech principally for that object, after bringing forward the evidence that I thought tended to prove that proposition, among other things, I went on with this little bit of comment, which I will read to you. I said this: we cannot absolutely know that all these exact adaptations are the result of preconception. But when we see a lot of framed timbers, different portions of which we know have been gotten out at different times and places, by different workmen—Stephen, Franklin, Roger, and James, for instance (Douglas, Pierce, Taney, and Buchanan), all collaborators in the conspiracy to nationalize slavery, and when we see these timbers together and we see they exactly make the frame of a house or mill, all the beams and mortises exactly fitting, and all the lengths proportions of the different pieces exactly adapted to their respective places and not a piece too many or too few, not omitting even the scaffolding, or, if a single piece be lacking, we can see the place in the frame exactly fitted and prepared; in such case, we find it impossible to not believe that Stephen and Franklin and Roger and James all understood one another from the beginning, and all worked upon a common plan or draft before the first lick was struck.

NARRATOR. As we know today, Douglas was the leader of this plot, this ill-conceived plan that set in motion the path to the Civil War. Douglas denies to the end that popular sovereignty had anything to do with the separation of the Union. Although in his defense, his ideas were so ingrained it blindsided his objective view.

DOUGLAS (*debate*). Now about this charge of conspiracy, Mr. Lincoln today goes on and quotes a part of his speech—a playful part of it—about Stephen and James and Franklin and Roger, etc. and said that I did not take exception to that and did not answer. He repeats it again. That was not what I took exception to. What I took exception to was this: afterward, he made a speech in which he said he intended that speech as a charge of corruption and conspiracy between the Justices of the Supreme Court, President Pierce, President Buchanan, and myself. *That gave the offensive character to the charge.* He then said that when we made it, he did not know whether it was true or not, but he said that inasmuch as Judge Douglas has not denied it, although he replied to the other parts of the speech three times, he now repeated the charge of the conspiracy on Judge Douglas and thus turned it into a charge of moral turpitude, and when he put it in that form, I did not say that inasmuch as he repeated the charge merely because I did not deny it—did it on my silence, not knowing it to be true. *I would deprive him of the opportunity of ever repeating it again by saying it is an infamous lie.* He says he will repeat the question until I will get into answering his folly about Franklin Pierce and Associate Justices Grier and Catron. All I have to say is, I am not green enough to let him make a charge and then take up the whole of my time in answering a charge, which I know to be false. Instead of putting myself on the proof and disproving it, I will say it is a lie! He (Lincoln) can attack my public record, my views, *but he cannot attack my moral integrity* by a charge of conspiracy between me and Justice Taney and two presidents. *I repel it!*

NARRATOR. As a willing or active, even on a subconscious, participant, all of the men named by Lincoln did set the stage for the Dred Scott Decision to be the worst in the history of the Supreme Court. Let's start with President Franklin Pierce. He was a pro-slavery man in his actions and proved them with his beliefs. He was a believer in States rights and their determining the existence of slavery. In the opening lines of his inaugural address, he says: "It is a relief to feel that heart but mine can know the personal regret and bitter sorrow over which I have been borne to a position so suitable for others rather than desirable for myself." At the persuasion of no less than Stephen

Douglas at a Sunday meeting, President Pierce signs the Kansas-Nebraska Act of 1854, which supersedes the 1850 Compromise Act. He continues to talk about the sectional divide over slavery; however, he does not want to abolish slavery. Early in his administration, he appointed John A. Campbell, a Southerner, to the Supreme Court, on the advice of the other sitting Justices. This was done with the intention of appeasing the Southern States. Justice Campbell concurred with Chief Justice Taney in the Dred Scott Decision. (*Hmmm, part of the plan to nationalize slavery?*)

PROFESSOR HARRIS. I would suggest at this point we should examine Justice Campbell's concurring option. He wrote a long and historical concurring opinion. Some of his points are well taken, and others were absurd.

JUSTICE CAMPBELL. I have endeavored to find a solution for the grave and difficult question involved in this inquiry. My opinion is that the claim of Congress of supreme power in the territories, under the grant to "dispose of and make all needful rules and regulations respecting the territories," is not supported by the historical evidence drawn from the Confederation or the deliberations, which preceded the ratification of the Federal Constitution. The Ordinance of 1787 depended upon the action of the Confederation, the Assent of the State of Virginia, and the acquiescence of the people, who recognized the validity of that plea of necessity, which supported so many acts of the governments of that time, and the Federal government accepted the ordinance (1787), which did not allow slavery in any new territory.

NARRATOR. This was also because slavery was to become extinct, to die of natural causes according to the Constitutional convention. Justice Campbell quotes from Gouverneur Morris in 1803, "I perceive that I MISTOOK the draft of your inquiry, which is substantially whether Congress can admit, as a new State, territory which did not belong to the United States when the Constitution was made. In my opinion, it cannot. I always thought when we should acquire Canada and Louisiana, it would be proper *to govern them as providences and allow them no voice* in our councils. In wording the third *section of the Fourth Article*, I went as far as circumstances would permit to establish the exclusion." Now let us look at the part President James Buchanan played in this plot to *nationalize slavery*. I again remind you that the Dred Scott Decision did just that: nationalize slavery. President Buchanan endorsed the Lecompton Constitution to admit Kansas as a slave State. This caused anger in the North. Douglas, in an unusual move, did not support the Lecompton (siding with the Republicans), opposing Buchanan. Douglas says it did not *express the principle of popular sovereignty*. Buchanan was in favor of the Kansas-Nebraska bill and popular sovereignty; however he was not in favor of the Dred Scott Decision. Buchanan was from Pennsylvania, as was Associate Justice Grier. He tried to convince Grier to dissent. Grier was communicating with president-elect Pierce and was convinced to agree with the majority. To conclude this investigation, I quote Lincoln in a speech he gave in July 1858:

> This is the repeal of the Missouri Compromise. The forgoing history may not be precisely accurate in every particular; but I am sure it is sufficiently so for all the uses I shall attempt to make of it, and in it we have before us the chief materials enabling us to correctly judge whether the repeal of the Missouri Compromise is right or wrong.
>
> I think, and shall try to show that it is wrong, wrong in its direct effect letting slavery into Kansas and Nebraska and wrong in its perspective principal, allowing it to spread to every other part of the whole world men can be inclined to take it.
>
> This declared indifference, but, as I must think, covert real zeal for the spread of slavery,

I cannot but hate. I hate it because of the monstrous injustice of slavery itself.

I hate it because it deprives our republican example of its influence in the world; enables the enemies of free institutions with plausability, to taunt us as hypocrites; causes the real friends of freedom to doubt our sincerity. And because it forces so many good men amongst ourselves into an open war with the very fundamental principles of civil liberty-criticizing the Declaration of Independence, and insisting there is no right principle of action but self-interest.

EPILOGUE

I feel that Lincoln was correct to form a more perfect union! This was the transition from the Articles of Confederation to the Declaration of Independence, the conclusive proof that the "old men," the authors of these documents, had the vision to include all, therefore not denying the Negro slave to share the dream of America.

The tragedy, of course, was the Civil War. Once the Civil War started, how did they resolve their remorse, or did they?

Justice Peter Daniel died on May 31, 1860. Chief Justice Taney did not resign from his position but thereafter would never be able to reclaim his reputation as an honorable man.

Justice John McLean died on April 4, 1861, at age seventy-six. It's possible that everything he did in his dissenting opinion in the Dred Scott Case might have contributed in his death.

Senator Stephen A. Douglas died in April 1861. To the end, he denied that his popular sovereignty was responsible for the war.

BIBLIOGRAPHY

Dred Scott v. Sanford. 60 US. 19; Howard 393; 15 L. Ed. 691 WL 8721; 1857 Lexus 472.

Goodwin, Doris Kearns. *Team of Rivals: The Political Genius of Abraham* Lincoln. New York: Simon & Schuster, 2005.

Holzer, Harold. *The Lincoln-Douglas Debates: The First Complete, Unexpurgated Text*. New York: HarperCollins Publishers, 1993.

Lubin, Martin. *The Words of Abraham Lincoln: Speeches, Letters, Proclamations, and Papers of Our Most Eloquent President*. New York: Black Dog & Leventhal Publishers, Inc., 2005.

Milton, George Fort. *The Eve of Conflict*. New York: Octagon Books, Inc., 1934.

Simon, James F. *Lincoln and Chief Justice Taney: Slavery, Secession, and the President's War Powers*. New York: Simon & Schuster, 2006.

ABOUT THE AUTHOR

I was born in Brooklyn and grew up in Baldwin, New York. I still live in Freeport, New York, where I raise my daughter. I graduated with a BS in history. When I attended college part time for many years, I became interested in the law, so I took a paralegal certificate program in 1990. Law, I realized, is related to history.

I took a course in political science. The way the class was set up, we had a mentor for each subject. We met every few weeks and discussed the topic and my assignment. I wrote a paper on the Bay of Pigs and one on the CIA. This was when I became interested in Supreme Court history.